APOLLO

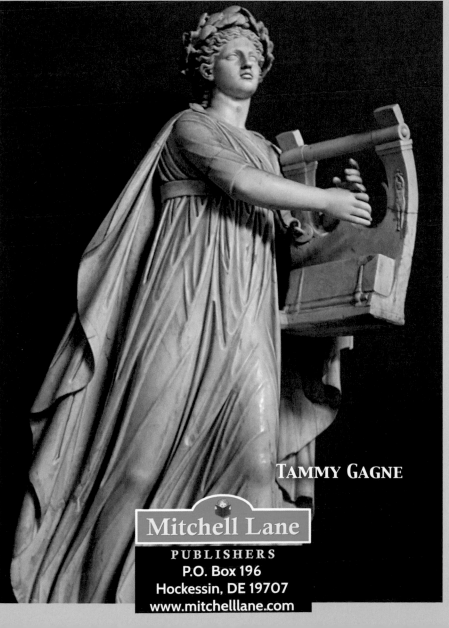

Tammy Gagne

Mitchell Lane
PUBLISHERS
P.O. Box 196
Hockessin, DE 19707
www.mitchelllane.com

Mitchell Lane
PUBLISHERS

Printing   1   2   3   4   5   6   7   8

A Kid's Guide to MYTHOLOGY

Apollo
Athena
Hercules
Jason

Odysseus
Poseidon
Thor
Zeus

Library of Congress Cataloging-in-Publication Data
Gagne, Tammy, author.
 Apollo / by Tammy Gagne.
    pages cm. — (A kid's guide to mythology)
 Audience: Ages 8-11.
 Audience: Grades 3-6.
 Includes bibliographical references and index.
 ISBN 978-1-68020-010-2 (library bound)
1. Apollo (Deity)—Juvenile literature. 2. Mythology, Greek—Juvenile literature.
3. Gods, Greek—Juvenile literature. 4. Mythology in literature—Juvenile literature.
I. Title.
 BL820.A7G34 2016
 398.20938'01—dc23
                                                                                2015005439
eBook ISBN: 978-1-68020-011-9

PUBLISHER'S NOTE: The Internet sites referenced herein were active as of the publication date. Due to the fleeting nature of some web sites, we cannot guarantee they will all be active when you are reading this book.

To reflect current usage, we have chosen to use the secular era designations BCE ("before the common era") and CE ("of the common era") instead of the traditional designations BC ("before Christ") and AD (anno Domini, "in the year of the Lord").

DISCLAIMER: Many versions of each myth exist today. The author is covering only one version of each story. Other versions may differ in details.

CONTENTS

Words in **bold** throughout can be found in the Glossary.

Apollo is known throughout the world as the Greek god of the sun, music, and poetry. This statue of the god stands at the site named for him—the Temple of Apollo—in Pompeii, Italy.

1
OLYMPUS, WE HAVE A PROBLEM

It was movie night at the Papadopoulos household. And the younger generation had a made a small wager. Nick had bet his older sister Taylor a week's worth of chores that the movie would be lame. It was their father's turn to choose the film. Last time, he had picked something that had been made before they were born. She took the bet, hoping that her dad's taste wouldn't strike out twice in a row—and even more hopeful that she wouldn't have to do the dishes this week.

As soon as their father returned with a pizza box in hand, Taylor begged, "Now will you tell us what we're watching?" Dad had a strict policy of secrecy when it came to unveiling his choices. The only thing he took more seriously than his pizza was his movies. And he loved surprising his family.

"I'll give you a hint," he teased, as he and their mother stacked plates and napkins on top of the cardboard box edged in blue Greek scrollwork before heading into the living room. Movie night was the only time the Papadopoulos clan ate in front of the television. And the Greek pizza that Dad always brought home from his favorite takeout restaurant made up for the movies he selected. "Houston, we have a problem," he said.

He sounded so serious that both teens instantly looked back, thinking he had dropped something. But then they realized the sentence was their hint.

Mom just smiled. Clearly she knew something Nick and Taylor didn't.

"Drumroll, please," Dad requested. But the kids simply rolled their eyes. "We're watching *Apollo 13* [uh-POL-oh]," he finally announced. "It's about the Apollo space program, specifically the seventh mission. Two days into the astronauts' journey to the moon, an oxygen tank exploded. It limited their communication with the people on Earth and threatened their return home."

"Wasn't Apollo a Greek god?" Taylor asked.

"He sure was," Dad replied. "The space program named the mission after him."

"Hey, I read about Apollo in school," Nick interjected. "He was the god of the sun, music, and something else. . . ."

"Poetry," finished Mom. "And healing, too." Dad knew his movies and his pizza. But Mom was the family authority on mythology. She wasn't Greek like their father. She just loved the ancient stories about the gods and goddesses. She had told Nick and Taylor many myths when they were younger. They made excellent bedtime stories.

The Meaning Behind the Myths

Mythology was the way the ancient Greeks explained how the earth and everything on and around it had been created. At this early point in history, people knew very little about science. The ancient Greeks gave Apollo credit for the sun rising each morning and setting each night. They believed that he pulled it across the sky with a chariot.

"So did the astronauts make it back?" Nick demanded, knowing full well that his father wasn't going to give away the movie's ending.

"Let's find out," Dad said as he popped the disc into the player. "Sounds like I made a good choice this time?" he asked and grabbed the remote control.

"Definitely," Nick replied, and then remembered his bet with Taylor.

"Don't worry. We're using paper plates tonight," she said holding hers up in the air. "You won't have to take over my duties until tomorrow."

Known as the king of all the Greek gods, Zeus is Apollo's father. The two do not always agree, however. When Apollo kills Python, Zeus bans his son from Olympus.

As the disc's previews launched, Nick couldn't stop thinking about Apollo. "Mom, did you ever tell us any of the myths about Apollo?"

"I don't think I did," she answered. "But you seem to know a thing or two about him yourself. Maybe you can tell me a story when the movie is over."

"Just make sure it's not too lame," Dad said and winked at their mother.

A Challenging Beginning

What Nick remembered most about Apollo was his birth story. Apollo's father was Zeus (ZOOS), the king of all the gods. His mother was the beautiful Leto (LEE-toh), the daughter of Titans Coeus (KEE-ohs) and Phoebe (FEE-bee). But Zeus was not married to Leto—his wife was Hera (HEER-uh). Nick also remembered that Hera was very jealous of Leto. She took her jealousy out on Apollo and his twin sister, Artemis (AHR-tuh-mis)—even before they were born.

Hoping that the twins would never be born, Hera forced Leto to live at sea. She demanded that no land allow Leto to enter. But when the soon-to-be mother arrived at the island of Delos (DEE-los), it welcomed her anyway, providing her with a place to give birth. It wasn't much of an island. It floated in the sea, pushed around by the wind and waves. But when it allowed Leto to stay there, four pillars grew from the ocean floor to hold the island in place forever.

Like many Greek myths, this earliest story about Apollo is an exciting one. Leto certainly isn't the only goddess to be banished by one of the gods. But when Apollo and his twin finally arrive, everything that his mother had to endure seems somehow worth it. Apollo's cry was said to be a sound of music. And like his mother, he was beautiful to the point of perfection.

Despite Hera's efforts, the other gods and goddesses welcomed Apollo and Artemis. Every one of them in fact gathered on the remote island to witness the twins' birth. The goddess of justice Themis (THEE-mis) fed the infants nectar and ambrosia (am-BROH-zhuh), the drink and food of the gods. One might say that this detail is symbolic—that she was making up for Hera's mistreatment of Leto.

Many of the gods came with gifts for the children. Zeus himself gave his infant son a chariot drawn by swans. When he was just four days old, Apollo received another item from Hephaestus (hi-FES-tuhs) for which he would be forever known: his bow and arrows. Although these may seem like odd presents for a newborn baby, bear in mind that the gods grew at a much faster rate than humans. Some came into the world fully grown. Within just days Apollo had grown into a strong and capable young god.

*Statue of Leto
with Apollo
and Artemis*

No Myth

The ancient Greeks believed that Zeus and the other gods and goddesses were real. They credited the gods with creating the earth—and they believed they still controlled much of what happened in the human world. Today, though, most people believe both the Greek gods and the stories about them are fictional.

Delos, however, was—and still is—a real place indeed. Named a UNESCO World Heritage site, the Greek island in the Aegean Sea draws its share of visitors. Legends state that no **mortals** would ever be born on the land. While this part of the story might make the destination unappealing to some people, the legends also barred any human beings from dying on the island either.

Long ago Greeks on Delos took the folklore so seriously that they escorted anyone who was seriously ill to the nearby island of Rineia. Even pregnant women were ushered away before giving birth. To prevent the sick from traveling to the island in hopes of recovery, modern Greeks have found a new way to help keep the legend alive. With no homes or hotels on Delos, no one lives—or even sleeps overnight—on the island.

Lion statues guard the Sanctuary of Apollo on Delos.

The Greek gods and goddesses have inspired many works of art. This 1688 painting by French artist Noël Coypel shows Apollo being crowned after killing Python and taking over the oracle on Mount Parnassus.

GREEK GOD—AND SHEEP HERDER?

Shortly after Apollo was born, he set out to establish an **oracle**. This would be the place where a human would go to learn about the gods' plans for the world— and then pass the information on to the rest of the people. Apollo chose a site on Mount Parnassus, but another oracle already existed there. Dedicated to Gaia (GUY-uh), the goddess of the earth, the oracle was guarded by her son, Python.

The snakelike creature had been killing the people who lived in the surrounding area. It had also been destroying their flocks of sheep. So when Apollo used his bow and arrows to fight the serpent, he became a hero to the people. Shepherds in particular were grateful to him for saving their pastures and flocks.

Even though the people were happy to be free of Python, Apollo would have to pay for his actions. For nine years, he was banned from Olympus. During this time he would serve as a shepherd for Admetus (ad-MEE-tuhs), the king of Thessaly, to make up for killing Gaia's son.

A New Beginning
Once Apollo had served his sentence for killing Python, he set up a new oracle in place of the old one on Mount

Parnassus and became its ruler. It was called Delphi (DEL-fahy), for an animal that was special to Apollo—the dolphin. Apollo even transformed himself into a dolphin upon his return to the oracle site.

The ancient Greeks embraced the sun god and began to celebrate the death of Python. The Pythian (PITH-ee-uhn) Games, consisting of art and athletic contests held every four years, were named in honor of the beast's death. The woman who spoke to Apollo at Delphi and passed his messages on was called the Pythia. Every eight years, another festival called the Septerion was held at Delphi. At this event, a young boy would set fire to a hut or a tent and then run away to the city of Tempe to be forgiven. This act represented Apollo's slaying of Python and his banishment.

One might say that Delphi is where mythology met the masses in the ancient world. It was the center of the Greek world, or as the Greeks called it, the *omphalos* (OM-fuh-luhs)—or navel. When someone had a question, big or small, he or she would travel there to find out the answer. People came from the far reaches of the Mediterranean Sea seeking guidance.

The Pythia, while not a goddess herself, appeared to have powers from another world. Before offering guidance to the people, she would chew on **laurel** leaves. She would sit over a crack in the earth, where fumes from the opening rose into the air. Breathing them would send the **prophetess** into a **trance**. It was at this time that the ancient people believed she was communicating with Apollo—and sharing his wishes with the human world.

The Pythia is depicted here in an oil painting by English artist John Collier. The 1891 piece, called Priestess of Delphi, shows the oracle seated atop her three-legged stool with laurel leaves in her hand, breathing in fumes from the earth.

Destination: Delphi

While most people in the world today agree that the Greek gods and goddesses were just characters in complex stories, Delphi—like Delos—is very real. Did the people who gathered at Delphi thousands of years ago actually hear the will of Apollo shouted out before them through a prophet? Or was the so-called prophet merely pretending to hear the gods? The prophet might have even imagined the conversations, truly believing they were happening. No one knows for sure. But many fans of mythology, as well as a smaller number of modern worshippers of these gods, travel to Delphi each year.

"The town of Delphi," writes journalist Toni Salama, "nestles in a narrow pass where small hotels on one-lane streets jostle one another to give guests a room that looks back down to the sea—and a valley populated with another three million or so more of Greece's olive trees."[1]

Not all of Delphi's treasures remain intact, but there is still plenty for visitors to see. Many sculptures and statues are kept at the Archaeological Museum of Delphi. Salama's favorite piece of art in the museum is the *Charioteer of Delphi*, "a bronze with features so realistic that even after 2,500 years the 5-foot-11 figure still gazes at the world through eyes of inset **onyx** (some say glass) framed by copper lashes. He originally would have stood in the temple of Apollo with a **brace** of horses—maybe four, maybe six—no longer here."[2]

The ancient Greeks built the Temple of Apollo during the seventh century BCE to honor their sun god. That structure was destroyed by a fire and the people rebuilt it. The new temple would stand for over a hundred years before an earthquake would eventually cause great damage

One of the most famous Ancient Greek statues is the Charioteer of Delphi, *created around 474 BCE. Its sculptor is unknown.*

All that remains of the Temple of Apollo today are ruins. Nonetheless, the damaged structure still attracts a fair number of visitors to Delphi each year.

to it as well. It was rebuilt yet again, but today that Temple of Apollo stands in ruins. "What's left of the Temple of Apollo are a half-dozen or so pillars indistinguishable in color and texture from the rocky cliff face behind," notes Salama.[3]

GIFTS OF LIFE AND LOVE

While Apollo served as Admetus's shepherd, the two formed a close friendship. The king treated Apollo well, a kindness that the god returned. Apollo showed his gratitude to Admetus by granting him a great favor: an extended life. Apollo promised his friend that on the king's deathbed, another could take his place.

Apollo also helped Admetus when the king fell in love with Alcestis (al-SES-tis). Her father would only allow them to be together if Admetus came for her in a chariot drawn by a lion and a boar. Using his divine powers, Apollo made it possible for the mortal king to fulfill these unusual wishes—and win the hand of his lady love.

But when the time comes for "another" to die in the king's place, Admetus learns that the nameless person is actually Alcestis. She is more than willing to give up her life for her husband. But Admetus is heartbroken.

This particular myth has been told and retold over time in many forms. One of the most popular ways is as a play titled *Alcestis*. "The bulk of the play is concerned with Admetus's dilemma," writes poet John Burnside. He goes on to explain, "On the one hand, for his people's sake, he must remain alive, to continue the golden age which his reign has brought; on the other, he cannot imagine living without his young wife, whom he loves deeply."[4] Thankfully for both the title character and her husband, Apollo saves the day at the last minute with the help of Hercules (HUR-kyuh-leez). The king and his wife are both saved from death.

Admetus is heartbroken as he stands beside his beloved wife on her deathbed.

A talented archer, Apollo is often depicted with his bow. This weapon that Hephaestus gave him soon after he was born also plays a part in many of the myths about the god.

GOD OF (NEARLY) ALL TRADES

New mythology students might define Apollo as the sun god. But others who have learned more about him realize just how many sides this **deity** had. The stories of his time as a shepherd made the ancient people see Apollo as the protector of all flocks and herds. He also retained his connection to dolphins. He was said to spend the winter months among the swans in the northern land of the Hyperboreans. Because of Delphi, Apollo was considered the god of prophecy. His bow and arrows—and his skill with them—linked him closely with archery. His wide range of interests and skills made him one of the most important Greek gods.

As the god of music and poetry, Apollo was the leader of the muses. These nine goddesses were his half-sisters. They were the children of Zeus and Mnemosyne (nee-MOZ-uh-nee), the goddess of memory. Each muse had the job of protecting a certain type of art or science. They encouraged humans to create poetry and dance, or to learn more about history and astronomy.

The Inspiration of the Gods

As an appraiser in Alameda, California, Jane Alexiadis often explains the meanings of historic works of art and estimates

from his command of music. The ancient Greeks believed that music had healing powers. They thought it purified both the body and the mind.

Many modern people—from Greece and elsewhere—agree. "A good diet of the right kind of music gives us mental, emotional, intellectual, and spiritual stability," states Aubrey Aloysius, director of the Lorraine Music Academy in India. "It brings people together, enhances our intelligence, academic achievement, creative ability and helps us to connect with our innermost being."[5]

Music has proved helpful to some of the most incredible minds of both ancient times and the modern era. Aloysius points out, "Ancient beliefs are returning to modern life and recent research has proven that learning music significantly improves memory, concentration, **spatial** thinking, creativity, and **linguistic** ability." Even though most schools tend to focus on math as a more important subject than music, Aloysius thinks that they are equally important in education.[6]

He states that the two subjects are linked as well. "Written music is based on the principles of mathematical progression. That is why most great scientists, mathematicians, astronomers, and artists, including Pythagoras, Claudius Ptolemy, Leonardo da Vinci, Albert Einstein, and Galileo, actively participated in music."[7]

Einstein seemed to especially benefit from learning to play the violin. "His poor performance in school caused Einstein's teachers to conclude that he was 'too stupid to learn,'" says Aloysius. "His parents bought him a violin at which Einstein became **proficient**. The way Einstein figured out his problems and equations was by **improvising** on the violin. Music helped bring out the genius in him."[8]

When Albert Einstein was a young child, his teachers could never have predicted that he would become one of the greatest thinkers in the world. On the contrary, they saw him as a poor student. The gift of music—learning how to play the violin—may have been what changed his future.

A modern illustration of Apollo's connection to medicine can be found in a common symbol for healing. The emblems of the American Medical Association, emergency medical technicians (EMTs), and the World Health Organization all feature the staff of Asclepius (uh-SKLEE-pee-uhs)—a rod with a single snake twisted around it. Asclepius was Apollo's son and also his student when it came to medicine and healing. The Association of American Medical Colleges explains, "One day Asclepius saw a snake crawl from a crack in the earth and entwine itself on his staff. Asclepius killed the snake, but immediately thereafter another snake emerged from the crack carrying an herbal leaf in its mouth; it placed the leaf on the head of the dead snake, which miraculously revived."[9]

From that point forward, Asclepius and the snake were inseparable. He continued to study medicine, and eventually became such a powerful healer that he was able to save many humans from death. This angered Zeus, who felt that only the gods should have the power to live forever. And so Zeus killed Asclepius with a bolt of lightning. But Zeus couldn't stop the people from continuing to ask Asclepius for healing. According to Doctor Keith Blayney, "Medical schools developed, which were usually connected to temples or shrines called Asclepions dedicated to Asclepius. The Asclepion became very important in Greek society. Patients believed they could be cured by sleeping in them. They would visit, offering gifts and sacrifices to the god, and be treated by priest healers (called the Asclepiadae)."[10]

Apollo's son, Asclepius, is shown here with his staff and snake.

APOLLO'S MUSES AND THEIR SPECIALTIES

Calliope (kuh-LAHY-uh-pee) was the muse of **epic** poetry. It is said that she inspired Homer to write the *Iliad* and the *Odyssey*. Drawings and paintings of Calliope show her holding his famous epic poems.

Clio (KLEE-oh) was the muse of history. She was so closely linked to her specialty that the ancient Greek word for history was actually *clio*. She holds a clarion (ancient trumpet) in her right arm and a book in her left.

Erato (ER-uh-toh) was the muse of love poetry. Even her name refers to love. The ancient Greek word for the feeling of falling in love was *eros*. She holds a a harp-like instrument called the lyre.

Melpomene (mel-POM-uh-nee) was the muse of tragedy. You will recognize Melpomene's image by the tragic mask that she holds.

Terpsichore (turp-SIK-uh-ree) was the muse of dance. Her name comes from the Greek word *terpo*, which means "amused." She holds a lyre as she dances.

Thalia (thuh-LAHY-uh) was the muse of comedy. The opposite of Melponeme, she created art that prompted laughter. She holds a mask of a laughing face.

Polyhymnia (pol-i-HIM-nee-uh) was the muse of sacred poetry, music, and dance. Polyhymnia sometimes holds a lyre, but she is always shown looking thoughtfully toward the sky.

Euterpe (yoo-TUR-pee) was the muse of lyric poetry. She was said to have invented several musical instruments. But the one she is seen with most often is a double flute.

Urania (yoo-REY-nee-uh) was the muse of astronomy. She is shown surrounded by stars, holding a planet-like sphere and a compass.

Apollo's most intense love was for a beautiful water nymph named Daphne. Sadly, Daphne would never return his great affection for her, thanks to the god of love, Eros. Here, she transforms into a laurel tree just as he catches up to her.

4

APOLLO'S BROKEN HEART

Like his father, Apollo had many loves—including both goddesses and humans. By far the most intense was Daphne (DAF-nee), a beautiful water **nymph**. From the moment he saw her, Apollo pursued Daphne with great enthusiasm. But his determination to win her heart didn't exactly come from his own.

Apollo was a skilled archer, and he wasn't always humble. He wasn't always kind either. After he made fun of Eros, the god of love, for his poor archery skills, Eros used his own talents to get even with Apollo for ridiculing him. First, he shot Apollo with one of his gold-tipped arrows to make him fall in love with Daphne. But to make sure that she would never return his affection, he dipped another arrow in lead. He shot the water nymph with this one, which made her refuse all of Apollo's advances. No matter where he followed her, she continued to flee from him.

Just when it seemed like Apollo was finally going to catch up with her, she evaded him once again. As he reached for her, Daphne turned into a laurel tree with the help of her father, the river god Peneus (puh-NEE-uhs). Still under the spell of the arrow, his intense feelings were then transferred to the laurel, which he made his sacred tree. Its leaves would later be used by the Pythia to foretell the future at Delphi.

More Love—And More Loss

Even when Eros wasn't interfering, Apollo's love life wasn't much better. Whenever he tried to win the affections of women, he was met with heartbreak in one way or another. After Daphne, Apollo fell in love with Hecuba (HEK-yoo-buh). But she was nearly as unavailable to him as the water nymph. She was already married to King Priam of Troy. Nonetheless, she fell in love with Apollo and together they had a son, Troilus (TROY-luhs).

The Trojan War is the setting for a number of myths, including this one. It begins when King Priam's son Paris seeks the love of Helen, who was the wife of the Greek king Menelaus (men-uhl-EY-uhs). Paris was more successful at love than Apollo, as Helen returned his feelings. However Menelaus was not willing to give up his wife without a fight, and the love affair triggered the ten-year war between the Greeks and the Trojans. A prophetess declared that the Trojans would win the war—as long as Troilus reached the age of twenty. When Achilles (uh-KIL-eez) killed him, Troy's hopes for winning the war died with him.

The next object of Apollo's affection was Cassandra, the daughter of Hecuba and Priam, and sister of Paris. When Apollo fell in love with the Trojan princess, he offered her the gift of being able to see the future. Although she accepted the gift, she wasn't really interested in the god. Apollo, hurt by yet another rejection, placed a curse on her so that no one would believe her predictions.

Toward the end of the Trojan War, the Greeks left a giant wooden horse outside Troy's city walls. The Trojans

Characters from Greek myths were depicted in many art forms. This jar shows Achilles grabbing Troilus by the hair as he tries to get away.

thought the Greeks had given up and gone home, and had left this gift as a peace offering. Cassandra could see that this horse would be very bad for Troy, and she begged the leaders not to bring it into the city. No one listened. Unfortunately for them, several Greek soldiers were hidden inside the horse. At night, they crept out and unlocked the city gates, allowing the entire Greek army to enter and destroy Troy.

English artist Evelyn De Morgan painted this image of Cassandra in 1898. The city of Troy burns behind her after the Trojans ignored her warning about the Trojan Horse.

Grown from Grief

Next, Apollo fell in love with the mortal Coronis (coh-ROHN-is). They lived together in happiness for a while. But according to Stanley Aronson of Brown University, "when he departed he left a white raven as her custodian. The raven later sought out Apollo, telling him that Coronis had fallen in love with another. Apollo's anger was so limitless that the raven's feathers turned black. And in rage, Apollo commanded his sister, Artemis, to slay Coronis with an arrow. As she lay dying, Coronis whispered that she was bearing Apollo's son."[1]

Not even the god of healing could reverse what he had done. "In desperation Apollo used all of his medical arts to try to save her life, but succeeded only in rescuing his infant son, named Asclepius. . . ."[2]

Apollo also had love affairs with men. But they were just as tragic as his relationships with women. Shortly after he fell in love with a prince named Hyacinthus (hahy-uh-SIN-thuhs), Apollo accidentally killed him with a **discus** while playing. Out of his grief, he created the flower called the hyacinth from his spilled blood.

Another young man who Apollo cared for died too young as well. This man, named Cyparissus (sih-puh-RIH-sihs), had tamed a deer that lived in a nearby forest. The animal became Cyparissus's pet and loyal companion.

One day while the boy was hunting boar, a bead of sweat trickled from his brow into his eye. The momentary distraction caused him to aim away from his target. His dart found its way to the deer instead. As his pet lay dying, Cyparissus was overtaken by his guilt. He begged Apollo to allow him to mourn the loss for all time. Immediately, his legs joined together and took root in the ground. His

In another version of the myth about Coronis, Apollo himself is the one who kills his mortal love upon learning that she has fallen in love with someone else.

skin was covered in bark, and branches that sprouted from him grew leaves. The tree that he became was known as the cypress tree, a symbol of mourning. The sap of the cypress tree forms in droplets on the bark, giving the appearance that the tree itself is crying.

ART INSPIRING ART

The stories of Apollo inspired many great works of art, including Giovanni Lorenzo Bernini's 1625 sculpture *Apollo and Daphne*. Journalist Sankha Guha discovered the statue during a trip to the Galleria Borghese (bawr-GEY-zee) in Rome. Guha is in awe of another one of Bernini's sculptures, *David*, when his attention—and breath—are taken away by the sight of Apollo and the object of his affection.

"Through a connecting door," Guha writes, "I catch sight of, possibly, the most thrilling piece ever wrought in marble, Bernini's *Apollo and Daphne*. I feel like Ben Stiller in *Night at the Museum*. I have the tingling sense of being in a forbidden place witnessing a forbidden scene. Daphne is caught in the moment she is transforming herself into a laurel tree to escape the attention of Apollo. Her skin is turning to bark; her fingers are morphing into delicate leaves that are blowing in the wind."[3]

Travel writer Rick Steves had a similar first impression of the piece. He calls the statue his favorite in all of Europe. He notes, "Bernini froze this scene at its most emotional moment, just as Apollo is about to catch Daphne and she begins to sprout branches from her fingers and roots from her toes. Apollo is in for one rude surprise."[4]

Apollo and Daphne *at the Galleria Borghese in Rome*

The artwork depicting Apollo is as diverse as the Greek god's own talents. This mosaic, a picture made from many tiny objects, was created during the fourth century.

FROM MYTH TO MODERN MARVEL

Apollo didn't always make the best choices. Despite being a god, he was far from perfect. For one thing, he made many mistakes. Some of them, as you've read, had tragic consequences. He also had a big **ego** and a bad temper. But sometimes his foolish temper caused a bit of comedy, too.

In addition to being a talented archer, Apollo was a gifted lyre player. He was even said to be the best. But his sister Athena (a-THEE-nah), the goddess of wisdom, was pretty talented herself. After finding a bone from a deer, Athena had carved out the inside and made several holes along the top. She found that when she blew into her creation, it made beautiful music.

Proud of her invention, which she called a flute, Athena played her music for the other gods and goddesses. Some merely giggled. Others told her that her puffed-up cheeks looked funny. Athena then ran to a forest, where she saw her own reflection in a stream. Embarrassed by what she saw, Athena threw the flute to the ground.

A young **satyr** by the name of Marsyas (mahr-SEE-uhs) then found it and began playing it. Unlike Athena, the creature who was half man and half goat didn't care how he looked, or if people laughed at him. He enjoyed playing the instrument and kept doing it. Over time he became quite skilled with the flute that seemed to have fallen in his path just for him.

An Ear for Music

Soon news of Marsyas's skill with his flute spread across the land. It even reached Apollo, who was upset by everyone's praise of the satyr. He decided to pay the creature a visit. When he arrived, he immediately challenged Marsyas to a musical contest. The satyr refused at once, admitting that the god was the greatest musician of all. But Apollo insisted. He wanted to prove that his talent was superior.

King Midas began organizing the event. And Apollo asked the other gods to serve as the judges alongside the king. Each musician played remarkably well, but Apollo was certain that he would be the winner. The judges clearly agreed—all except for Midas, that is. When the king insisted that Marsyas should be the winner, Apollo was enraged. He decided that the problem must be that Midas's ears were not big enough to hear properly. With that, the king's ears were turned into huge donkey ears.

This myth is likely the inspiration behind the name of the famous Apollo Theater in New York City, as well as countless others around the globe. As arts and music editor Barry Didcock puts it, "From Harlem to Glasgow via Sheffield and London, there can't be a city in the English-speaking world which doesn't have an Apollo theatre."[1]

An Epic Experience

Apollo himself remains a popular character in the modern world, appearing in books, films, and even comic books. In recent years Rick Riordan's Percy Jackson book and movie series especially have taken the teenage world by storm. University of Wisconsin English professor and author Liam Callanan learned that his daughter Honor really enjoyed the series. So much, in fact, that she wanted to see the setting firsthand.

The Apollo Theater in New York City was named after the Greek god Apollo. Although it may be the best known, it definitely isn't the only venue named for the god of music.

"Mr. Riordan's books, which follow the fictional children of the Greek gods as they roam the modern-day world," writes Callanan, "have inspired a wave of adolescent fascination in ancient myths and the characters who populate them. They spurred Honor to explore the subject more deeply—she was surprised to learn that the author didn't create all the mythology in the books, while I was taken aback that he'd placed Mount Olympus atop the Empire State Building. And they prompted me to plan a week-long trip to Greece as an educational adventure."[2]

Parts of the trip were more exhausting than he expected. But in the end, Callanan wasn't at all sorry. "My eleven-year-old daughter had decided that the best way to experience ancient Olympia—a sprawling riverside complex in Greece where the Olympic Games were held starting in the eighth century BCE—was to run the roughly two-hundred-yard track that Zeus's son Hercules supposedly laid out. Under the scorching midday sun, was it a smart thing to do? No. Did it make [ancient times] come alive in a rush that I can feel again typing these words? Ye gods, yes."[3]

The Callanans especially enjoyed visiting the site of Apollo's oracle. The trails leading to Delphi on the slopes of Mount Parnassus were steep and twisting. "Because we arrived in late afternoon, we had the site, lighted with **gossamer**-gold late-day light, all to ourselves. Fittingly, our destination was another temple to the sun's charioteer, Apollo. Only about six stumpy, wind-worn columns remain, but that made it easy to see the view beyond—which seemed to [include] all of Greece. Zeus is said to have [sent] two eagles to find the center of the world; Delphi was where they connected. No argument from us."[4]

Knocking Down Barriers

In the modern world, Apollo has become a **trailblazer** of sorts. Appearing in both DC and Marvel, he has been found on comic book pages since the 1970s. His DC character is among the first openly gay comic book heroes. The original myths about the Greek god tell the story of a god with little luck in relationships. Most of his love interests either reject him or die. But in the world of DC Comics, Apollo finally settles down. In 2002, he and fellow DC character Midnighter get married and adopt a superhero child. They assume the job of raising Jenny Quantum after her mother is murdered.

The Escapist magazine explains how writer Mark Millar broke down an important barrier for gay couples. "Rather than tone down the relationship between Apollo and Midnighter, he made it one of the [series's] central themes. What made it more remarkable, at least to people used to seeing gay characters treated like afterschool specials or the subjects of Very Special Episodes, is that they were treated for the most part like just another loving couple, albeit with parties who happened to have incredible super powers."[5]

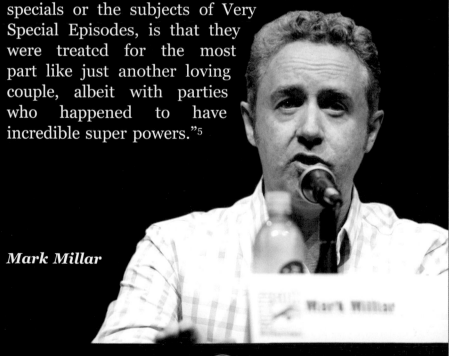

Mark Millar

Chapter 2: Greek God—and Sheep Herder?

1. Toni Salama, "The Greek Classics: 3 Sites of Legend Reveal the Reality Behind the Lore," Mcclatchy—Tribune News Service, September 15, 2008.

2. Ibid.

3. Ibid.

4. John Burnside, "In Giants' Footsteps," *Scotsman*, October 30, 1999.

Chapter 3: God of (Nearly) All Trades

1. Jane Alexiadis, "Chromolith of Muses Spans Centuries," *Contra Costa Times*, February 18, 2012.

2. Lee Siegel, "Where Have All the Muses Gone?" *Wall Street Journal*, May 16, 2009, http://online.wsj.com/articles/SB124242927020125473

3. Ibid.

4. Ibid.

5. Aubrey Aloysius, "Ancient Wisdom to Today's Rescue," *New Indian Express*, September 11, 2011, http://www.newindianexpress.com/magazine/article360703.ece?service=print

6. Ibid.

7. Ibid.

8. Ibid.

9. Association of American Medical Colleges, "1987-88 Annual Report," p. 9, https://www.aamc.org/download/374958/data/ar_1987-1988.pdf

10. Keith T. Blayney, "The Caduceus vs the Staff of Asclepius (Asklepian)," September 2002, http://drblayney.com/Asclepius.html

CHAPTER NOTES

Chapter 4: Apollo's Broken Heart

1. Stanley M. Aronson, "The Origin of a Sacred Oath," *Providence Journal*, June 14, 2004.

2. Ibid.

3. Sankha Guha, "When in Rome, Don't Do as the Tourists Do. Start Your Sightseeing Early," *Independent*, February 26, 2012, http://www.independent.co.uk/travel/europe/when-in-rome-dont-do-as-the-tourists-do-start-your-sightseeing-early-7440787.html

4. Rick Steves, "In Rome, Feeling the Power of the Baroque," *Toronto Star*, April 12, 2014.

Chapter 5: From Myth to Modern Marvel

1. Barry Didcock, "The Myths That Live on in Language," *Sunday Herald* (Scotland), October 23, 2005.

2. Liam Callanan, "A Percy Jackson-Inspired Family Trip to Greece," *Wall Street Journal*, July 18, 2014.

3. Ibid.

4. Ibid.

5. Ross Lincoln, "Good Riddance, Fred Phelps: 5 Pivotal Moments For LGBTs in Comics," *Escapist*, March 21, 2014, http://www.escapistmagazine.com/articles/view/comicsandcosplay/11168-Good-Riddance-Fred-Phelps-5-Pivotal-Moments-For-LGBTs-In-Comics.5

WORKS CONSULTED

Alexiadis, Jane. "Chromolith of Muses Spans Centuries." *Contra Costa Times*, February 18, 2012.

Aloysius, Aubrey. "Ancient Wisdom to Today's Rescue." *New Indian Express*, September 11, 2011. http://www.newindianexpress.com/magazine/article360703.ece?service=print

Associated Press. "Rings and Things." *Grand Rapids Press*, August 13, 2004.

Association of American Medical Colleges. "1987-88 Annual Report." p. 9. https://www.aamc.org/download/374958/data/ar_1987-1988.pdf

Blayney, Keith T. "The Caduceus vs the Staff of Asclepius (Asklepian)." September 2002. http://drblayney.com/Asclepius.html

Bowman, Laurel, Anthony Bulloch, Andrew Campbell, Alys Caviness, Kathryn Chew, and Anna Claybourne. *Gods and Goddesses of Greece and Rome*. New York: Marshall Cavendish, 2011.

Burnside, John. "In Giants' Footsteps." *Scotsman*, October 30, 1999.

Buxton, Richard. *The Complete World of Greek Mythology*. London: Thames & Hudson, 2004.

Callanan, Liam. "A Percy Jackson-Inspired Family Trip to Greece." *Wall Street Journal*, July 18, 2014.

Didcock, Barry. "The Myths That Live on in Language." *Sunday Herald* (Scotland), October 23, 2005.

Guha, Sankha. "When in Rome, Don't Do as the Tourists Do. Start Your Sightseeing Early." *Independent*, February 26, 2012. http://www.independent.co.uk/travel/europe/when-in-rome-dont-do-as-the-tourists-do-start-your-sightseeing-early-7440787.html

Hamilton, Edith. *Mythology: Timeless Tales of Gods and Heroes*. New York: Warner Books, 1969.

WORKS CONSULTED

Lincoln, Ross. "Good Riddance, Fred Phelps: 5 Pivotal Moments For LGBTs in Comics." *Escapist*, March 21, 2014. http://www.escapistmagazine.com/articles/view/comicsandcosplay/11168-Good-Riddance-Fred-Phelps-5-Pivotal-Moments-For-LGBTs-In-Comics.5

Mutén, Burleigh. *Goddesses: A World of Myths and Magic.* Cambridge, MA: Barefoot Books, 1997.

Napoli, Donna Jo. *Treasury of Greek Mythology.* Washington, DC: National Geographic, 2011.

Philip, Neil. *The Illustrated Book of Myths.* New York: DK Publishing, 1995.

Salama, Toni. "The Greek Classics: 3 Sites of Legend Reveal the Reality Behind the Lore." Mcclatchy—Tribune News Service, September 15, 2008.

Siegel, Lee. "Where Have All the Muses Gone?" *Wall Street Journal*, May 16, 2009. http://online.wsj.com/articles/SB124242927020125473

Steves, Rick. "In Rome, Feeling the Power of the Baroque." *Toronto Star*, April 12, 2014.

FURTHER READING

Holub, Joan, and Suzanne Williams. *Heroes in Training: Apollo and the Battle of the Birds.* New York: Aladdin, 2014.

Pearson, Anne. *Eyewitness Ancient Greece.* New York: DK Publishing, 2007.

Temple, Teri. *Apollo: God of the Sun, Healing, Music, and Poetry.* Mankato, MN: The Child's World, 2013.

GLOSSARY

brace (BREYS)—two of a kind; a pair

deity (DEE-i-tee)—a god or goddess

discus (DIS-kuhs)—a round heavy disk that is thrown for distance in a sporting event

ego (EE-goh)—self-importance; self-image

epic (EP-ik)—describes a long poem about a hero

gossamer (GOS-uh-mer)—thin and light, resembling a thin fabric or cobweb

improvise (IM-pruh-vahyz)—to perform or create without preparing or planning ahead of time

laurel (LAWR-uhl)—a European evergreen tree with dark green leaves

linguistic (ling-GWIS-tik)—related to language

mortal (MAWR-tl)—one who will not live forever; a human

nymph (NIMF)—a lesser goddess, usually on earth, not in the heavens

onyx (ON-iks)—a stone containing visible bands of different colors

oracle (AWR-uh-kuhl)—the place where a Greek god answered questions through a human; can also refer to the human giving the message or to the message itself

philosophy (fi-LOS-uh-fee)—the study of the basic ideas about knowledge, truth, right and wrong, religion, and the nature and meaning of life

proficient (pruh-FISH-uhnt)—skilled at a particular science, art, or subject

prophetess (PROF-i-tis)—a woman who speaks on behalf of a god or tells the future; the message she gives is called a prophecy

satyr (SEY-ter)—a forest god who is half human and half goat or horse

spatial (SPEY-shul)—referring to physical space

trailblazer (TREYL-bley-zer)—someone who creates a path where there was not one before, allowing others to follow; a pioneer

trance (TRANS)—a state in between sleeping and waking, in which it was believed that a person was able to receive messages from a god

INDEX

ABOUT THE
AUTHOR

Tammy Gagne is the author of numerous books for adults and children, including *Athena* and *Thor* for Mitchell Lane Publishers. She resides in northern New England with her husband and son. One of her favorite pastimes is visiting schools to speak to kids about the writing process.